CITY PARK
NEW ORLEANS

Magnificent Balance of Art, Nature & Play

CITY PARK
NEW ORLEANS

*Magnificent Balance
of Art, Nature & Play*

photography by Kerri McCaffety
text by Kerri McCaffety
with Mikko Macchione

published by Vissi d'Arte Books for
Friends of City Park

First Edition
Text Copyright 2013 by Kerri McCaffety with Mikko Macchione
Photographs Copyright 2013 Kerri McCaffety (except where noted)
All Rights Reserved
Book Design: Kerri McCaffety and Cynthia Reece McCaffety
    with John Hopper, City Park Chief Development Officer and Public Affairs Director

Published by Vissi d'Arte Books for Friends of City Park

www.neworleanscitypark.com   www.friendsofcitypark.com

Library of Congress Cataloging-in-Publication Data

McCaffety, Kerri.
  City Park New Orleans : magnificent balance of art, nature and play / Kerri McCaffety. -- First edition.
      pages cm
    Includes index.
  ISBN 978-0-9709336-9-0 (hardcover)
  1. City Park (New Orleans, La.)--Pictorial works. 2. City Park (New Orleans, La.)--History 3. New
Orleans (La.)--Pictorial works. 4. New Orleans (La.)--History. 5. New Orleans (La.)--Buildings struc-
tures, etc. 6. New Orleans (La.)--Social life and customs. I. Macchione, Mikko. II. Title.
    F379.N57C575 2013
    976.3'35--dc23
                                        2013035479

Printed in Korea

Cover Photo: The iconic Peristyle and lions, 1907

End Sheet Photo by John Hopper

Page 8: The Butler Fountain, bronze statue of a water nymph, *Chloe*, 1929

Page 10: Popp Fountain, 1937

Page 11: Detail of the gondola on Big Lake

Page 13: Jester, City Putt miniature golf course, 2013

Page 14: Detail of the Dueling Oak

Page 17, 22-23: photos by John Hopper

Contents

Acknowledgments

It is impossible to say what a wonderful experience it has been to photograph and write about City Park, a place I have loved for decades and which holds many profound personal memories. Instead of being excessively sentimental, I hope this book will show what I can't say.

I want to thank the administrators of City Park, those who championed it through the years, volunteers and donors who make this urban Eden part of our great city. Especially, thank you to William Hoffman, Robert Becker, John Hopper, Julie La Cour, Paul Soniat, eagle-eye editor Linzey Powers, golf pro Kai Yee, disk golf guru Michael Kernan, gondolier extraordinaire Roberto Dula, and Louisiana Wildlife and Fisheries guys (biologists) Shane Granier and Jarrod Galloway.

John Hopper acted as co-artistic director for the planning and design of this book and helped any time I needed. Mikko Macchione helped greatly with the vast amount of research and writing. We relied on many resources for historical information, especially the *History of City Park New Orleans* by Sally K. Evans Reeves and William D. Reeves, published in 1982.

Thank you,

Kerri McCaffety

Foreword

City Park New Orleans: A Magnificent Balance of Art, Nature, and Play, is a loving assembly of photographs and stories depicting the astonishing landscapes of this historic park and the people and activities which give the landscape life.

For nearly 160 years, since its founding in 1854 with a gift from philanthropist John McDonogh, City Park has been the heart of the recreational and cultural life of the New Orleans region. Gradually expanding to 1,300 acres when the last piece of property was acquired during World War II, the history of the park is intricately connected with that of the city. Through good times and bad, the park has been the place where New Orleanians have come to recreate, relax, learn, participate in and revel in the unparalleled beauty of the oaks and other landscapes.

Certainly the park has faced its challenges. It is an ironic note of history that the two greatest periods of park development and redevelopment have followed two of the nation's greatest tragedies—the Great Depression and Hurricane Katrina. Both of these events led to long periods of renewal and progress, with the park experiencing its latest rejuvenation after the devastating destruction of Katrina.

The photographs contained in this book serve as a reminder of both the magnificent beauty of the park and its man-made contributions, which give millions of annual visitors an enriching and engaging experience in this beautifully verdant setting. Change is a constant theme in the park, as illustrated in photographs of the historic live oaks and new gardens, the park buildings from the Peristyle to the new City Park/Pepsi Tennis Complex, the historic WPA Botanical Garden and the lagoons and waterways, as well as special events such as Celebration in the Oaks and the Voodoo Music Experience.

It is the sincere hope of the board and staff that this book will serve as a constant reminder of the treasure which is City Park. While the images that could be in this book are endless, photographer and writer Kerri McCaffety has created a book that captures the essential qualities of this great Park. She has done a terrific job. We hope you enjoy the photos and stories.

Finally, we want to recognize the board and staff of City Park for their stewardship of this great resource and the countless volunteers, donors and friends who have contributed to the park's recovery and renaissance since Katrina. We thank you!

William D. Hoffman, President
Robert W. Becker, Ph.D., Chief Executive Officer
The City Park Improvement Association

History Part 1: A Soft Nuisance
From Land Grant to Municipal Dairy Farm

New Orleans sits where it does because the Vieux Carré is slightly above sea level and lies between Lake Pontchartrain and the Mississippi. Conveniently for the original French developers of the area, the Esplanade Ridge was an above-sea-level route connecting both bodies of water. Early settlers surely noticed the large shady tract of cypress, magnolia and live oaks fronting Bayou St. John and it wasn't long before the area became the city's first farmland.

Almost immediately after Bienville founded the city in 1718, François Héry was granted the property and retained it for half a century. The property eventually came to his granddaughter, Francisca Lorreins, and her husband, Jean Louis Allard, and would be known for many years as the "Allard Plantation."

Allard and his brother grew corn and sugar and raised cattle and sheep. By the early 19th century, he had an impressive complex of buildings on his plantation. The surveys of the time show Allard held the land that would become the modern corner of the park containing the New Orleans Museum of Art and extending east to encompass all of the present-day Fairgrounds racetrack. Poignant tales survive of Allard mortgaging his holdings to finance a crop that never yielded benefit, and in 1845, New Orleans investor/philanthropist John McDonogh bought the property at a sheriff's sale for about $40,000. McDonogh, a shipping magnate who owned a swath of the West Bank across from New Orleans, was an eager real estate maven.

Many accounts of the sale tell of McDonogh allowing Allard to stay on the property and two years later, when Allard died, having him interred in a crypt on the grounds. A crypt, described by locals as Allard's, did rest in the shade of the surviving Dueling Oak for over a century and a half while rumors swirled that it was actually empty. In 2011, after electronic imaging proved that there was indeed no Monsieur Allard, or any other occupant, in the crypt, it was removed.

McDonogh, a reclusive and peculiar figure in New Orleans lore, proved himself to be one of the city's great heroes when his will dictated that his vast wealth be split evenly between his home town of Baltimore and his adopted town of New Orleans, to be used for schools. After all the legal wrangling, it worked out to a nifty sum of more than $700,000 for each community.

As a part of this legacy, the city inherited the land that would become City Park. McDonogh had suggested in his will that cultivating the area with smaller farms could accrue more income for the city. However, in the early 1850s, New Orleans experienced something rare in its history—it was swimming in money. This "progressive and permanent prosperity" prompted local leaders to look to more aesthetic issues. The city was growing and with it demands for urban improvements—including pleasing greenspaces. In addition, the local press singled out the swampy area along Bayou St. John as a "nursery of disease" and campaigned for it to be cleared and drained to mitigate the mosquito annoyance, and even proposed that it be converted into a public park.

Life, even in a rich, vibrant port city such as New Orleans, could not have been particularly healthful. Muddy, animal-ridden streets, congestion, smoke and other toxins emanating from the constant traffic of ships, disease, noise, dust and oppressive heat all contributed to a growing concern for the quality of life in inner cities, not just in the Crescent City, but across the nation. In the mid-19th century, a national movement arose to create urban oases, or as landscape architect pioneer Frederick Law Olmsted espoused, to create in the heart of urban areas "pleasure grounds" that would screen out the cacophony of city life and restore residents to a sense of natural harmony. He designed Central Park in New York, which opened in 1858. Lincoln Park in Chicago (1860), Forest Park in St. Louis (1876), Golden Gate Park in San Francisco (1880), and many others in almost every urban center soon followed.

As early as 1852, through the efforts of Mayor Abdiel Crossman and city surveyor Louis Pilié, the Common Council of the municipalities approved a plan to lay out a park on the old Allard Plantation. It would be almost ten years before any actual work could be done on creating the park, but it was a start.

During the Union occupation of New Orleans in the 1860s, residents were already availing themselves of the cooler area on the city grounds. Though they had to compete with cattle that still roamed there, visitors would ride the transit line from the old city up Esplanade Avenue to the bayou and picnic out on the greens. In fact, in 1863, Union military men organized a large outdoor festival on the grounds, with flags flying, schoolchildren singing, and ladies conversing with soldiers. This served for a bit of propaganda to show the nation how peaceful and lovely New Orleans was under federal care.

The McDonogh Oak, named for John McDonogh, is one of the oldest of City Park's ancient trees, estimated to be more than 800 years old.

Ralph's On The Park, one of the city's most elegant restaurants, occupies the 1860 building that was the coffee house of Jean Marie Saux.

Just before the war, Jean Marie Saux, a French immigrant, built a refreshment stand across from the park and tended it for years. It is the location today of the restaurant Ralph's on the Park. Saux complained bitterly of the cattle running amok on the park, chasing away his customers. In court he stated, "You cannot move in the park without stepping in the soft nuisance prepared in the night by the cows." This particular nuisance serves as a fitting metaphor for the challenges that lay in the next thirty years to the growth of the park.

Once the Civil War was concluded, and no more soldiers were interested in having fêtes on the lawn, none of the previous affluence remained. Carpetbaggers seeped into government, opportunists skimmed money from every public project, and in the atmosphere of bald-faced corruption, political acrimony crippled any progressive public action. These events caused a beleaguered populace almost to forget the park. At one point, for seemingly lack of any better ideas, the unfortunate Monsieur Saux was engaged by the city to take care of the cows.

To make matters worse, New Orleans' "other" City Park, today's Audubon Park, was chosen as the site for the Cotton Centennial Exposition—the 1884 World's Fair. This enormous project drew away precious resources and attention from the area. Help arrived in the 1890s, when a tireless visionary florist who grew up in the neighborhood decided to take a stand for "Old City Park."

Trees Without Equal Anywhere In The World

The Southern Live Oak, *Quercus Virginiana*, grows all over the Gulf South, but the largest stand of mature specimens flourishes at City Park. Because the trees lose and replace their leaves throughout the year and appear evergreen, they are called "Live Oaks." More than 30,000 trees grow in City Park, of which 2,500 are live oaks. Some of the more famous of the trees are the McDonogh Oak and the Anseman Oak, both over 600 years old. Another well-loved tree, which lost its brother to a hurricane in the 1940s, is the Dueling Oak. The Dueling Oaks were the legendary meeting place of affronted Creoles and Americans who came out to the solitude of the area to defend their honor. As one paper wrote, "Blood has been shed under the old cathedral aisles of nature."

The official State tree, the bald cypress, loses its needles every year. Cypresses populate the islands and ring the waterways of the park. Another solid Southern image, Spanish moss, drapes languidly from oak, cypress and crape myrtle branches all over the park. The moss, an epiphyte, does not harm its host tree.

In 1866, the *New Orleans Times* called City Park's oak and cypress trees "the most beautiful that grow ... without equal anywhere in the world," musing that they might even have been here when Bienville mapped out the city. In fact, the oldest trees in the park today are around 800 years old and were substantial before Columbus started his voyage to find India. These ancient oaks began their lives when Genghis Khan was invading China, Crusaders were slaughtering the Infidels, and the Anasazi Indians were carving cliff dwellings in the mountains of southwest Colorado.

Above: The Dueling Oak, famous site of many *affaires d'honneur*. From Colonial days throughout the 19th century, dueling was so prevalant among wealthy Creoles that it had its own set of laws, called the *Code Duelo*. The smallest insult could easily result in defense of honor by swords or pistols. Dueling in the park was outlawed in 1890. Only one still survives of the twin trees traditionally known as the Dueling Oaks.

Right: For generations, New Orleans children have climbed the park's old oaks.

History Part 2: Fête Champêtre
The Father of City Park and Something to Celebrate

The genesis of the park that is so loved today comes from the vision of a retired nurseryman who grew up just down the street. But the early going was a lot more arduous and tedious than simply planting trees and landscaping flowers.

Victor J. Anseman's childhood home was on Metairie Road, called City Park Avenue today. While most people would relax into a tranquil retirement, he tirelessly cajoled politicos, judges, businessmen, engineers and others until finally he forged a committee, the City Park Improvement Association, in 1891. Today, visitors enjoy a range of elaborate and simple diversions, but Anseman and his committee had more mundane concerns to address. Waterways were stagnant, brush overgrown, trees needed attention, roads were laughable, access to the park was difficult, original plantings from fifty years earlier had been neglected to barrenness ... and, of course, the darn cows.

One of the first orders of business for the association was to build a fence. As is pointed out in other histories of the park, the fences contained the cattle, but they also defined the park. The ornamental Hinderer's iron fence was constructed along with a gate to the Alexander Street (now Anseman Avenue) entrance. It must have provided great hope and inspiration to the committee to see in glorious golden letters, "New Orleans City Park," over the gate. That hope would have to fuel them; at that point they had little else.

The original main entrance to City Park was on Alexander Street where a gate known as Hinderer's Gate previously stood in 1892.

The Pizzati Gate now arches over the old entrance. Built in 1910, the iron gate was a donation from steamboat captain Salvatore Pizzati, a Sicilian who immigrated to New Orleans and made his fortune in the local shipping industry.

Bayous had to be dredged, shells (which were used as gravel) had to be layered on the roadways, greenswards cleared, bridges built, and a clean, natural ambience restored. George Grandjean, committee member and civil engineer, laid out plans for roadways and a rejuvenation of the waterways. Eventually, a clear, inviting lagoon was dug with fresh water pumped in from Bayou St. John. The day they opened the valve for the first time was occasion to create a typical New Orleans gala. Slowly, the park was regaining its local allegiance. But paying for the improvements was Anseman's constant quandary.

The park received income from picnicker rentals of tables; concessions fees; permit charges; selling surplus trees, ducks, geese, and lumber; growing and selling hay; and believe it or not, leasing a back area for the grazing of cattle. Finally, five years into the commission's labors, a state appropriation was passed whereby the park could get funds for its maintenance.

In 1892, the park imported a French idea that anticipates today's Jazz Fest down to the time of year—the *fête champêtre*. This "country feast" was in reality an ambitious garden party. The day would kick off with baseball on the old Allard sugar field, then cakes, ice cream, and beer followed as folks would enjoy a marching band competition. A hot-air balloon might take off from the same field, and over on the new lagoon would be the heart-stopping skiff races. After a parade, visitors might find a quiet spot to nap. They would need it.

Facing Page: The 1902 Langles Bridge, named for Angele M. Langles. Ms. Langles and her mother died on July 4, 1898, when the French steamboat *La Bourgogne* sank after colliding with a British ship in the North Atlantic.

Facing Page, Top: Goldfish Bridge, built abound 1902, leads to Goldfish Island, across Bayou Metairie from the Peristyle. Bottom: The 1902 Pichot Bridge, a rough-hewn cobblestone bridge dedicated in the memory of Henrietta M. Leonie Pichot.

The first carousel in City Park operated in 1897 powered by mules. In 1898, the miniature train began operation. Both traditions continue over a century later.

In the gloaming, orchestras and singers would perform from the bandstand. Also on the stand would be puppet shows and other extravagances. A night parade, sometimes on the water, would follow. By 1897, the park had its mule-driven carousel and a year later, the miniature train debuted. The first golf course opened in 1902 and was the only one in the city. When the Peristyle, still the park's most famous icon, was completed in 1907, folks would dance under the Greek temple décor until almost midnight. And the whole thing wrapped up with fireworks.

The dawning of the new century gave park supporters much to celebrate. Mayor Paul Capdevielle also happened to be the park board president, meaning many city projects coincided with advancing the park's cause. For example, he orchestrated street improvements that allowed easier access to the park. In addition, not only did local railroad companies open lines direct to the park, but they sponsored outdoor concerts there.

The concerts must have been a hit, because the park committee invested in chairs, music stands, and charming electric lights strung from poles replacing smoky, smelly oil lamps. Soon there were concerts every Sunday and Wednesday evening followed by a presentation featuring the exciting new invention—the graphoscope. Also known as a "vitascope," it was an early hand-cranked motion picture projector. For the first two decades of the 20th century, the park hosted free motion pictures. This attraction, in the form of free summertime movies, survives to this day.

The Peristyle, built in 1907, is still the park's most famous icon. Originally intended for dancing, the Peristyle was designed by architect Paul Andry and was called the *paristyleum*.

In 1907, the dedication of the Peristyle was celebrated with music and fireworks, just as events like the park's "Third of July" is today.

With all these activities, visitors would need a place to sit and have lemonade. The Casino, an example of Spanish Mission Revival architecture, was built in 1912 and served as a refreshment stand and administrative center for City Park. Although technically a "cantina" (a place where refreshments are served), as the story goes, the strong local accent transformed the word into "ca-sin-a" and eventually "casino." It was never a gambling establishment.

Sculptor Pietro Ghiloni carved the four concrete lions that guard the Peristyle.

The Spanish Revival Style "Casino," now Morning Call Café, opened in 1912 to serve refreshments downstairs and to house park administration offices upstairs.

Popp Bandstand, 1917

Concerts became so popular at the park, and so lucrative as sponsors picked up the tab, that finally they installed a permanent Greek-columned bandstand. Lumber magnate John F. Popp donated funds for the Popp Bandstand. He wanted a site to harmonize with the Peristyle just down the road. Musical presentations were a staple of the park right through the 1960s, and today there is an encouraging comeback of live music events.

The musical events, the special galas, the improved access to the park, and most importantly, the rejuvenation of public appreciation for the park all propelled it toward its modern incarnation. The park's early successes are directly traceable to the indefatigable dedication of the men and women who saw a jewel in the festering tract; and for good reason, the man who spearheaded that renaissance, Victor J. Anseman, is known as the "Father of City Park."

The Anseman Oak and Bridge, named for Victor J. Anseman, the "Father of City Park."

Isaac Delgado's Sweet Deal

New Orleans Museum of Art

At the midway point of the 1800s, when teenaged Isaac Delgado came to New Orleans from Jamaica, Louisiana annually produced around 100,000 tons of sugar cane. By 1900, when Delgado was nearing retirement as a sugar broker, 5 million tons of sugar a year poured out of the port city. Delgado and his uncle Samuel, with whom he lived, invested their fortunes wisely. They not only forged a sugar empire in the city; they were ubiquitous on the boards of banks, arts and social societies.

Samuel and his wife passed away within a year of each other and, having no children, left their nephew even more wealth. As he himself amassed a treasure trove of precious art pieces, it must have made sense to Isaac to create a museum, not only to keep his collection safe, but to share it with the citizens of the town he clearly loved.

After conversations with his good friend and committee member Paul Lelong, Delgado wrote a letter to the park board basically saying if they provided him a suitable site, he would donate "The Isaac Delgado Art Museum." New Orleans has historically been sensitive to its standing as a "great city," and news of an honest-to-goodness fine arts museum, which would add to local reputation, resounded through the city with great anticipation.

In 1911, at one end of Lelong Avenue, came the grand opening of what would come to be called the New Orleans Museum of Art. The Chicago firm of Lebenbaum and Marx modeled the building on Greek-Revival themes with grand Ionic columns and giant urns on the edges, but modified it with, as they stated, "a subtropical appearance." They probably meant the Spanish sloping green tile roof and glass panels above, as well as the tropical plants that often adorned the approaches.

Arriving from Esplanade Avenue, visitors come around the Beauregard Statue, pass through the Monteleone Gates, donated by the great local hotelier Antonio Monteleone in 1913, to travel the stately boulevard to the museum, which still overlooks Big Lake. Despite the occasional changes in floral disposition along the way, either through fiat or hurricane, it remains the most jaw-dropping entrance to the park.

Almost immediately, the museum collection grew to importance with donations from Delgado's estate, as well as from important art collector Benjamin Morgan Harrod; the estate of Chapman Hyams, whose wife, Sara Lavinia, also allowed for the building of a memorial fountain to the children of New Orleans; and a surprise donation of bronzes from French Quarter hairdresser Eugene Lacosst.

Though the Depression threatened the museum's existence, it persevered and was happy to accept an amazing collection of Old Masters paintings from Samuel Henry Kress, owner of the popular department store on Canal Street. As decades changed and the public's perception of art with them, the museum strove to expand its collection in many areas.

A watershed exhibit of Tutankhamen's Treasures was greeted by local giddiness in 1977. Almost a million visitors came to Lelong Avenue, now painted "Nola Nile" blue, to see the ancient Egyptian glories. To mark the 2003 bicentennial of the Louisiana Purchase, "Jefferson's America & Napoleon's France" brought another million or so visitors to the museum, and it seemed the city was eager to honor not only the great president, but also the emperor it once revered.

The museum expanded its exhibit space in a clever and wonderful way for local pedestrians when it opened the Besthoff Sculpture Garden. (The Besthoffs, a great local family of philanthropists, were the "B" in the seminal New Orleans pharmacy chain K & B.) The garden, a picturesque walk, contains works by Henry Moore, Fernando Botero, Barbara Hepworth, and fifty other world-renowned artists.

Isaac Delgado came to New Orleans and benefitted greatly from the sugary riches here. With a spacious expansion, an active social mission, a supereminent café run by bold restaurateur Ralph Brennan, and nationally important exhibits, it has become clear that Delgado's vision birthed an outstanding museum befitting a great city.

These 25-foot marble pylons mark the Esplanade Avenue entrance of City Park and were erected in 1914 in memory of park commissioner Antonio Monteleone. The pillars feature eight bronze lamps and 600-pound capstones.

At the Esplanade Avenue entrance to the park, in front of the Monteleone Gate, stands General Pierre Gustave Toutant Beauregard astride his horse. The bronze sculpture, resting on granite from Stone Mountain in Georgia, was created by Alexander Doyle in 1915 for $22,000. This statue is part of a trilogy of Confederate heroes sculpted by Doyle in New Orleans, the other two being Robert E. Lee in Lee Circle and General Albert Johnson in Metairie Cemetery. Doyle also created the statue of New Orleans' benefactor Margaret Haughery on Prytania Street, claimed by some to be the first statue to a female philanthropist in the country.

Beauregard was born in Louisiana of Italian and French parents, grew up speaking French, and had a distinctly Mediterranean look to him. He distinguished himself as an engineer and officer in the Mexican-American War. Upon returning to New Orleans, he was the superintendent engineer and successfully stabilized the construction of the enormous Customs House on Canal Street. He dipped his toe into political waters and was narrowly defeated when he ran for mayor of the city in 1858. When Louisiana seceded from the Union he became a general in the Confederacy. He commanded the troops that fired the first shots of the war at Fort Sumter, and again at the first battle of Bull Run, which was a rousing Southern victory. Because of his heritage and his military successes, some called him "Napoleon in Gray."

A man of many talents, Beauregard is credited with inventing a contraption that extricates ships from sandbars, and a type of cable car for urban service. It was this second invention that probably served him best, as after the war he ran a couple of different railroad companies. However, he made his real fortune when he became the president of the Louisiana Lottery in 1877. He passed away in his home, now museum, across the street from the Ursulines Convent in the French Quarter. Though his given initials were P. G. T. Beauregard, he often signed his own correspondences simply "G. T. Beauregard," and that is how his name appears on his stately memorial today.

1919 McFadden Mansion

In 1909, a gentleman by the name of Fred Bertrand built a simple five-bedroom house in woods near the park. Ten years later, Texas oil tycoon William Harding McFadden rebuilt it into a magnificent seven-bedroom palace, to go with his other homes around the country. The house featured a ballroom, trophy room, oriental garden, sunken garden, and marble swimming pool. As the park grew around him, McFadden sold his home to the park for $160,000. Legend has it that the ghost of a heartbroken lover named Lisa can be heard crying in the house. In 1960, the Christian Brothers opened their boys' school for 5th through 7th graders on the gorgeous grounds.

Above: Mr. Felix J. Dreyfous was one of eight New Orleanians who played a vital role in the development and nurturing of City Park in its earliest years. Dreyfous spent decades working to improve City Park, writing the park's original charter and the legislative bill for park funding, and creating and serving on NOMA's board of trustees. Mr. and Mrs. Felix J. Dreyfous donated the Dreyfous Avenue Bridge in 1924, replacing a wooden bridge.

Bottom Right: The *Colombier de Carol,* or pigeonnier, was designed by Felix Dreyfous and donated to the park in 1928. It stands on Pigeon Island behind the Casino Building.

On City Park Avenue near N. Hennessy Street in the Old Grove is another favorite icon of the park from 1929, the bronze statue of a water nymph, Chloe in the Owen/Butler Memorial Fountain. She originally held a pair of long, brass trumpets. The first fountain and sculpture on the site in 1910, *Unfortunate Boot*, was a memorial for William Frazer Owen, Jr., donated by his parents. In 1994, the fountain was restored in honor of Patrick J. Butler.

Popp Fountain, built in 1937, is 60 feet wide. At its center, a cast-bronze sculpture of leaping dolphins, designed by Enrique Alférez, sprays a 30-foot fountain. It is surrounded by 26 Corinthian columns. The park's Arbor Room has Popp Fountain as a majestic front yard.

As the nation struggled to extract itself from the Great Depression, City Park found itself in a very peculiar place. On one hand, its tract of land now stretched all the way from City Park Avenue to the lakefront, and the board of directors enlisted a prestigious national firm to design an ambitious megapark. On the other, there was virtually no money to go ahead with the developments.

Using a bequest from Mrs. Rebecca Grant Popp and her sister, Isabel, the park had the Chicago architectural group Bennett, Parson and Frost lay out a sprawling plan for the 1300-acre expanse that included a stadium, a system of lagoons, two golf courses, bridges, roads, tree maintenance, and beefed-up infrastructure—all emphasizing an irregular, pleasant aesthetic. Though they would not have used the term then, it was important to the guardians of the park that it have an organic, natural feel. But even while they ironed out the intricacies of a grand scheme, they had not a cent with which to proceed.

Two WPA bridges in City Park depict Enrique Alférez's image of a floating woman in bas-relief. This bridge, behind NOMA near Christian Brothers School, is unique in depicting both the floating woman and hand tools.

History Part 3
Works Progress Administration & Big Changes

Nationally, the Roosevelt administration was creating an alphabet soup of agencies designed to resuscitate the torpid economy and create jobs. Through diligent organization and planning by local leaders, significant federal money was attracted to the City Park cause. By 1935, Congress approved almost $5 billion for the Works Progress Administration—perhaps the most famous of the government projects of the time. In its eight years, the WPA built the Griffith Observatory in Los Angeles, Dock Street Theater in Charleston, Merritt Parkway in Connecticut, and similar accomplishments in almost every county in the country.

City Park would have been an attractive project for the WPA: its administrators favored landscape projects and public improvements because they employed a lot of laborers. Also, Louisi-

ana Senator Huey Long was a real political threat to FDR in the upcoming election of 1936, and the President privately admitted he backed relief programs—even modeling them on ones Long created at home—"to steal [Long's] thunder." To support a noble project right in Long's own backyard must have appealed to Roosevelt.

With the support of the WPA, more than 20,000 men found work over a six-year stretch, and close to $13 million was appropriated for improvements. Many stunning improvements had been merely a wish list only a few years earlier: City Park Stadium with its impressive Art Deco gates and enclosing fence; ten-plus miles of winding lagoons and set-off islands with eight new bridges; three other bridges totally redone, along with the paving of the major roadways; the Rose Garden—which would become today's Botanical Gardens and its inspiring statuary; two golf courses and many attendant buildings, including a plantation-style clubhouse designed by local architect Richard Koch; a maintenance area and mule stables known as "the Corral;" sidewalks, benches, and other fine-tuning improvements; and a colossal underground drainage, gas and water network.

In addition to the structural importance of the park facilities, there remain today the artistic touches that remind visitors of the vision of the park as an urban respite. Enrique Alférez, a Mexican-born artist who adopted New Orleans and had fought with Pancho Villa in the revolution, was put in charge of the WPA sculpture projects in City Park. His Art Deco figures and concrete-relief works populate the park, and under his guidance many of the bridges and structures bear insets appropriately memorializing the tools and hands of labor. This seems fitting, as most of the WPA workers completed the park projects by hand.

The Works Progress Administration's 20,000 workers built many bridges depicting workers and tools. They also built structures like the rose garden arches in the Botanical Garden..

Facing Page: In the rose garden, Schriever Fountain, Enrique Alférez, 1932, carved limestone

Above, Top: WPA structures and sculpture in the rose garden

Bottom: WPA bridge on Diagonal Drive

In 1937, President Franklin Delano Roosevelt himself, in a convertible limousine with Mayor Robert Maestri and Governor Richard Leche, came to City Park after a luncheon at Antoines to dedicate the mall named in his honor. From a time when New Orleans, and indeed the entire country, lived in desperate hope for economic relief, it seems almost miraculous that the foundations and landmarks of City Park erected then still endure and are beloved today.

Above: Many marathons and fun-runs begin or end under the cathedral of live oaks on Roosevelt Mall, including the Crescent City Classic and the Color Run.

Right: Six WPA Federal Eagles line Roosevelt Mall.

The Agony and the Ecstasy
Tad Gormley Stadium

Just north of the busiest part of the park, right off Marconi Drive, sits a plot of land that has witnessed every passion, from the bitterest acrimony and piercing sadness, to inspiring dedication and achievement, to the heights of religious- and even teenaged-girl-ecstasy. The site of Tad Gormley Stadium had once been a dairy farm, and through the machinations of a visionary, or con-man, depending on which version of the story one chooses to believe, it became an ambitious horse-racing complex.

City Park Race Track opened in 1905, and despite the Fairgrounds being just a few furlongs away, the track was a success. The developers planned an enormous hotel resort, and completed a free train shuttle—a bit bumpy, said the local newspaper *Item*, reporting that there was "a sag here and there"—to the imposing Grandstand. Not formally part of the park, the New Orleans Jockey Club had runaway profits for three whole years. In 1908, an anti-gambling governor amidst a rancorous public debate shut down all horseracing across the state.

With seating, a three-level grandstand, and a train line out from downtown, the track was still used for large events. In 1906, the order of the Knights of Pythias, a benevolent society, had its national jamboree of sorts, where thousands of participants paraded by the grandstand over an extended week. Air shows were also gaining in popularity. Air speed and altitude records were broken annually there. On New Year's Eve, 1910, daredevil flyer John Moisant took flight in his Bleriot monoplane from the racetrack's midfield off to Kenner to begin a 300-mile journey. While landing, at 25 feet, his plane caught a gust of wind and plummeted to the ground, killing him. In his honor, New Orleans' airport would be named Moisant Field, and though today it is Louis Armstrong International Airport, its identifying code remains "MSY."

The end of horse racing not-so-secretly relieved the park board members. Not only did the idea of gambling split them as a group, the negative press must have depressed the famously conservative members. Finally, and most importantly, the track impeded park expansion. Eventually, through the workings of five-time mayor Martin Behrman, the park acquired the land. By 1920, the park had doubled its size, gotten out of debt, and entered a great period of physical expansion that culminated with the arrival of the Works Progress Administration.

The WPA converted the track into magnificent City Park Stadium. Designed by architects Richard Koch and Julius Dreyfous, it featured a grand horseshoe with seating for 26,500 spectators, a cinder track-and-field course, and a football gridiron. In October 1937, the stadium debuted with a college tilt between now-forgotten football powers Loyola and DePaul. The high-school games afterward (Jesuit vs. Holy Cross and Warren Easton vs. Fortier) were better-attended, and to this day, high school football is the mainstay of activity at the stadium.

Besides football, a former prizefighter from Boston came to coach young people in track and field. He had started training athletes as early as the beginning of the century, and his first pupil won the 1904 Boston Marathon. Francis Thomas Gormley came to New Orleans to coach athletics at Loyola and LSU. He was a coach on the 1932 U. S. Olympic team. In 1938, he brought his popular "Gormley Handicaps," a series of amateur races, to City Park Stadium, where he was now athletic director. For years he volunteered his time to young runners for these informal Sunday morning track meets. In 1958, the city celebrated his fifty years of coaching service, and when he died seven years later, there was no voice that spoke against renaming the field "Tad" Gormley Stadium.

Other sporting highlights took place in the stadium's past, as well as a notable lowlight. The ill-fated New Orleans Pelicans, victims of a national disinterest in Minor League baseball, had their swansong—two miserable seasons—at the field before folding their wings for good. On the other hand, the promising American Football League, a few years before merging with the NFL, held an exhibition between the Boston Patriots and the Houston Oilers to show that New Orleans could be a viable professional football town.

In 1992, when the Olympics were to be held in Barcelona, a climatically similar location to New Orleans, the U. S. Olympic Track-and-Field Trials were held at the stadium. Coach Tad no doubt smiled down on the proceedings, as athletes strove under the motto, "No Pain, No Spain."

The stadium, history would prove, was not only a platform for athletic competition. Archbishop Joseph Rummel staged a gigantic Eucharistic Congress, a Catholic event that would draw close to 70,000 worshippers from across the country for a four-day weekend in 1938. Significantly, all races were welcome to celebrate the religious event, and it became one of the first major nonsegregated events in the city. Xavier, a historically Black Catholic university, hosted many of the week's events.

In other nonsporting highlights of the stadium's history, local-born movie star Dorothy Lamour sold war bonds; Roy Rogers and Trigger led a March of Dimes parade; and, perhaps most beloved to local memory today, the Fab Four added a stop at the stadium to their national tour in 1964.

At a whopping five dollars a ticket, thousands of delirious fans, mostly high-school girls who skipped afternoon classes to make their way to the park, crammed into the stadium to see, if not hear, the Beatles. When John, Paul, George, and Ringo appeared, after opening sets by Frogman Henry and Jackie deShannon, about 500 crazed young females stormed the fences in front of the stage, to be barely held back by courageous cops. No Beatle was harmed.

The Botanical Garden functions today as the esthetic heart of City Park. Designed by local architect Richard Koch, laid out by landscaper William Wiedorn, and decorated by sculptor Enrique Alférez, the WPA built infrastructure, cultivated specimens and added tasteful touches of art.

After World War II, the Rose Garden (as it was then called) and its beds of over 750 varieties of roses provided inspiration for a new generation of horticulturists. However, postwar neglect, challenging weather, and vandals took a toll on the garden until the early 1980s, when the Friends of City Park decided to take action. They raised money to fence in the garden including two impressive gates, one by the revered Alférez, almost fifty years after his WPA work establishing the garden.

A Poem in Flora
The Botanical Garden

In 1982, twelve fenced acres including the old Rose Garden and the conservatory was renamed New Orleans Botanical Garden, and a full-time professional horticulturist was hired. The next decades would see the garden blossom into an urban Eden and vibrant center of events and activities.

The Botanical Garden mixes lovely walks through parterre gardens, educational areas with indoor and outdoor exhibits, and an artistic repository of natural and man-made attractions. Floral walks spread out under charming pergolas, indoor gardens shelter cacti and succulents, organic produce gardens demonstrate their possibilities, and, of course, the rose gardens flourish. In all, over 2,000 species of plants thrive in the garden.

Above: Water Goddess, Enrique Alférez, 1930s, cast stone

Right: Reclining Nude, Enrique Alférez, 1932, carved limestone

Facing Page: *Adam and Eve*, Enrique Alférez, cast stone

This Page, Top: White Angel Trumpet flowers in the Botanical Garden

Above: Walking Iris

Facing Page: One of the pair of Alférez's *Satyrs on Poles*,
1932, cast concrete, at the entrance to the rose garden

The centerpiece building of the Botanical Garden is the Conservatory of Two Sisters with its stately glass dome, containing an indoor rainforest exhibit and a living fossil area. Surrounding the conservatory is sprawling lush greenery, flowers for every season, fountains and statuary. Nearby are a butterfly walk, an aroma garden, and a hummingbird garden.

The classical area is the Original Garden, containing the Lord and Taylor Rose Garden, lily pond, Garden Study Center, and the lovely Lath House. Further along, the Zemurray Azalea and Camellia Gardens, which include ostentatious magnolias, as well, showcase Louisiana's fragrant blossoms.

The demonstration garden rotates projects for education and aesthetic enjoyment. This area features original cold frames, the raised-brick gardens originally built by the WPA, used for the propagation of annuals to display in the park. Here local fruits, vegetables and herbs are grown and local horticultural issues explored.

Facing Page: In front of the Conservatory of the Two Sisters is a sculpture in cast concrete, *Undine,* by Rose Marie Huth, 1942.

The conservatory features a Living Fossils exhibit of prehistoric plants and a tropical rainforest exhibit.

Facing Page: Conservatory of the Two Sisters, Photo by Studio Tran

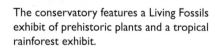

One of the goddesses of the garden, *The Flute Player*
by Enrique Alférez, 1995, bronze

Facing Page: *The Flute Player* surrounded by candles and flowers for a wedding
Photo by Studio Tran.

Above: Across the lawn from the Flute Player's fountain is the Haspel Outdoor
Stage, named for Robert B. Haspel, where City Park presents many concerts.

Top: Woman in a Huipil, Enrique Alférez, 1981, bronze

Bottom: *Renascence*, Enrique Alférez, 1998, cast stone

Facing Page: The Southern Shade Garden

Above: The Butterfly Walk
Left: Louisiana Iris

The exotic *Yakumo Nihon Téien* is a secluded Japanese garden honoring the Japanese name of writer Lafcadio Hearn. Japanese gardens are more abstract than Western gardens, and the effect is a poem in flora, rock and sand.

Delightfully hidden near the Japanese garden is an unlikely place to learn about the rest of city. The Historic New Orleans Train Garden features G-gauge replicas of local trains and streetcars running over 1,300 feet of track. Designed and built of botanical materials by model-train genius Paul Busse, the trains pass by tiny replicas of the different historic neighborhoods of the city and its landmarks.

Top: The Yakumo Nihon Téien Japanese Garden

Bottom and Facing Page: The Historic New Orleans Train Garden
photos on bottom right and facing page courtesy of City Park

Without a doubt, the most enduring memories of the Botanical Garden for many people will be of a function at the Pavilion of Two Sisters. Modeled after an *orangerie*, a special greenhouse considered de rigueur for any 19th-century estate, the pavilion features floor-to-ceiling arched doors, a flagstone dance floor, and stunning views of the surrounding garden. Locals recently voted the pavilion as the best place, out of so many intensely romantic choices in New Orleans, to have a wedding.

The burgeoning of the Botanical Garden exactly parallels the growth of City Park in the public attitude, from a lovely diversion for the mid-century citizen, to an integral social role in the psyche of a great modern city.

The Pavilion of the Two Sisters, named for Miss Erminia Wadsworth and Mrs. Marion Wadsworth Harvey.

Above, Top: One of the many lawns of the Botanical Gardens, surrounded by wondrous trees, including "Cascade Falls," or weeping bald cypress. Bottom: Orange cuphea

Facing Page: *Children on a Glide*, Jean Seidenberg, 1962, bronze

The Carousel Gardens and Storyland

Sara Lavinia Hyams left her jewelry to the two major New Orleans parks in 1914 for children's areas. It must have been some bling, because the proceeds provided for fountains, statues and a wading pool in each park. Many generations of locals remember wading in the pool at City Park, where the Hyams Fountain welcomes guests to the Carousel Gardens and Amusement Park.

The Hyams Fountain at the entrance to the Carousel Gardens.

With its hand-carved horses, Bavarian band organ, and lovely octagonal house, the carousel itself has been a fixture in the park since 1906 when it replaced an earlier mule-driven ride. It is one of only 100 antique wooden carousels in the country and the only carousel of its kind in Louisiana. The carousel was designed by acclaimed carvers Looff and Carmel and features 30 jumping horses and 21 standing horses, three menagerie animals and two chariots. The carousel is listed on the National Register of Historic Places.

Today the carousel is surrounded by other more modern rides and the station for the miniature train.

Top photo on this page courtesy of City Park

Many generations of New Orleans children remember their first
ride on the "flying horses" and the excitement of the annual Easter
egg hunt at the Carousel Gardens Amusement Park.

The miniature train carries on the tradition that began in 1898 and is a favorite attraction, especially during Celebration in the Oaks, when the lighted train speeds through acres of colorful decorations.

Other rides in the Carousel Gardens Amusement Park include a ferris wheel, bumper cars, Tilt-A-Whirl, monkey jump, and many more.

photos this page courtesy of City Park

Next to the Carousel Gardens is the star of the show for kids: Storyland. Conceived in the 1950s, this wonderland walk has classic wood-and-fiberglass sculptures of familiar fairy tales, from Mother Goose to Louisiana's own Colleen Salley's *Epossumondas*. Story times amuse the kiddies, and it's not unheard-of for grownups to rent the area for their own fun.

The THREE Little pigs

Nothing says Christmas in New Orleans like the magical mix of twinkle lights and Spanish moss hanging from the massive live oaks in City Park.

A small event that began in 1984 as "A Tribute to a Christmas Tree" has evolved over the years into a favorite New Orleans Christmas tradition. The nationally-famous "Celebration in the Oaks" welcomes more than 100,000 visitors a year. The month-long attraction gives guests cozy nights of stunning lights, choirs, Santa Claus, the adorned miniature train ride, and hot chocolate.

City Park's crew of seven lightscapers spend eight months each year designing, maintaining and installing over a million lights to create 24 acres of glittering dreamscapes in the Botanical Garden, Carousel Gardens, and beyond to light the peristyle chandelier, the trees in the Old Grove, all along the train tracks, and throughout the lagoons.

Old classics like the Loch Ness Monster and Santa's Pirogue are joined by new fanciful designs such as holiday flamingos and jingle jellyfish, plus high-tech, computerized LED displays including animated leaping frogs and baby dinosaurs hatching out of eggs.

Above: Treasure Island is a thirty-foot pirate ship in the lagoon, with cannon-fire sound effects, a mermaid, and a treasure chest full of gold.

Facing Page: The Cosmic Dancing Tree near the rose garden drips with LED lights like falling snow.

Facing Page, Top: A unicorn made of lights frolics in the Hyams Fountain at the entrance
to the Carousel Gardens. Bottom: The tree, named for artist Enrique Alférez, dances with
a computerized LED display synchronized to music.

Below: The Rose Garden dressed up for the holidays

Above: The colorful lights of Celebration in the Oaks reflect off the lagoon and outline the branches of the oaks in the Old Grove.

Facing Page, Top: Holiday Flamingos on Pigeon Island
Bottom: Glowing baby dinosaurs play on the lawn known as Dreyfous Meadow.

Run, Sweat, and Gears: Sports at City Park

City Park is alive with athletic activities. From children climbing, sliding, and swinging in playgrounds to bikers, joggers, and skaters zooming by to flying frisbees, tennis balls, and footballs, the action is constant. And like the traditions of picnics, concerts, and amusements, sporting activities at the park have thrived since the beginning.

The first gentlemen's sport in City Park may have been dueling, but many others soon followed. Baseball debuted at the *Fête Champêtre* in 1892. The park's first golf course opened in 1903 and was the only course in town. City Park tennis courts opened in 1928.

The Pan American Stadium was built in 1973 as the popularity of soccer expanded. Today the park also has the Matt Savoie Soccer Complex and fields, a softball quadruplex, golf driving range, baseball diamonds, football, rugby and lacrosse fields, two running tracks, four miles of bike paths, and several playgrounds.

City Park/Pepsi Tennis Center, one of the best tennis complexes in the state, offers 26 lighted courts (16 hard courts and 10 clay courts).

The 4,000-seat Pan American Stadium is home of the New Orleans Jesters, a USL Premier Development League soccer team. The stadium also hosts high school football games, soccer leagues and concerts.

Horseback riding in City Park has come a long way since the first pony rides in 1906. The stables, arenas and other facilities of the equestrian center cover 27 acres in the north part of the park on Filmore Avenue.

The New Orleans Police Department also has its stables in the park on Harrison Avenue.

In 2010 City Park introduced a 5,000-foot, 18-hole disc-golf course wrapped around the Little Lake area for frisbee fans. Disc golf is one of the newest sports in the park, while fishing might be even older than dueling, especially if we consider the Native Americans who lived around Bayou Metairie (now City Park's lagoons) before Europeans settled Louisiana.

With more than 11 miles of lagoons, City Park has plenty of places to cast a line, and the park has stocked its waters with bass since 1907.

City Park's Big Bass Fishing Rodeo started in 1946, and many generations later, the City Park big-bass record is over 9 pounds.

The wilderness areas of Couturie Forest and Scout Island offer sports like a ropes course and canoeing.

All over the park, fishermen can cast their lines from bridges, banks, or piers.

A Glorious New Century for City Park

As City Park's third century dawned, great new developments unfolded. The Couturie Forest Nature Trail and Arboretum opened in 2000. Philosophically, City Park sprang from the idea that every urban area needed a green retreat. Hikers in the 60-acre Couturie Forest, in the heart of the park off Harrison Avenue, not only get a retreat, they may forget they are in a city at all. Many of the trails are constructed from reclaimed materials from former park structures. The forest also boasts New Orleans' highest peak. Towering at 43 feet above sea level, Laborde Mountain is named for Ellis Laborde, beloved park manager from 1950 to 1978.

City Park's wild side, Couturie Forest Nature Trail and Arboretum, opened in 2000. (Photo above by Kaye Florane)

In contrast to the forest's virtually untouched wilderness, the Sydney and Walda Besthoff Sculpture Garden opened in 2003. More than 60 sculptural works valued at over $25 million spread over five landscaped acres behind the New Orleans Museum of Art.

Facing Page: Works in the Sydney and Walda Besthoff Sculpture Garden. In the foreground: *Overflow XI* by Jaume Plensa, 2008, stainless steel

This Page: The sculpture garden is a magical place with bridges, bayous and art. Rising out of the bayou are (top) *Virlane Tower* by Kenneth Snelson, 1981 and (bottom) *Pablo Casal's Obelisk* by Arman, 1983, bronze.

This Page, Top: *Tree of Necklaces*, 2002, by Jean-Michel Othoniel, glass and stainless steel. Bottom: The miniature train passes through the Dreyfous Meadow near the entrance to the sculpture garden and works by Alexander Calder.

Facing Page: The sculpture garden also features *Corridor Pin, Blue* by Coosje van Bruggen and Claes Oldenburg and *Riace Warriors I, II, III, IV* by Elisabeth Frink.

The Master Plan for 2018

In the first few years of the new millennium, City Park already had the twin jewels of the culturally significant Sidney and Walda Besthoff Sculpture Garden and the vast wilderness of Couturie Forest in its crown. And even greater things were on the horizon.

In March 2005, after considerable study and input from the public, the board approved a $115-million master plan designed to make New Orleans City Park the premier urban park in the nation with improvements in almost every area of the park as well as brand new developments in art, nature and play. The master plan is called "City Park 2018," for the 300th anniversary of the founding of New Orleans, and consists of more than 50 projects.

Big plans for City Park 2018 included the Goldring-Woldenberg Fountain and Great Lawn (above) and Big Lake, surrounded by 25 acres of recreation. (facing page).

The deluge and subsequent devastation wrought by Hurricane Katrina transformed City Park's dreamscapes into a nightmare. (photos this page courtesy of City Park)

After the Storm
A Silver Lining

City Park's ambitious new master plan faced a grave challenge when the failure of the federal levee system following Hurricane Katrina in 2005 left 95 percent of the park sitting in floodwaters for weeks, inflicting $43 million in damages to the park alone. Storm damage and subsequent revisions increased the cost of the $115 million plan to $153 million.

Legions of locals and businesses opened their wallets and volunteered their time not only to repair, but to enhance, City Park. The great storm brought echoes of the Great Depression and turned a terrible disaster into an unexpected outpouring of benefits for the park.

Plans went ahead for majestic improvements like Big Lake, the Festival Grounds, the Goldring-Woldenberg Great Lawn, and much more. Everywhere in the park today are the exciting new developments of the master, plan blending beautifully with the WPA-era sculptures, the turn-of-the-century Greek-Revival edifices, and the ancient trees.

A two-piece metal sculpture, *Grateful Labors*, was created for the park by Wayne Amedee in 2009 as a tribute to the people who helped in the ongoing recovery of the city post-Katrina.

Big Lake, with its 40-foot fountain shooting a plume of water into the sky, was completed in 2009. Visitors can rent boats or bikes, fish, jog, birdwatch, ponder artwork, or simply sit under the tranquil Singing Oak and listen to the music of the wind chimes in its branches.

On the shores of Big Lake is the Singing Oak, a creation of local artist Jim Hart. The giant tree is strung with a set of wind chimes that ring a pentatonic (five notes per octave) scale. One of the chimes on the Singing Oak stretches 14 feet.

Facing Page: An authentic Italian gondola actually imported from Venice moves as gracefully as the swans and brings Big Lake a bit of Old-Word romance.

Below: Photo by John Hopper

The Goldring/Woldenberg Great Lawn was completed in 2010. Three acres of grass stretch from the Peristyle on Dreyfous Avenue to the Storyland entrance on Victory Avenue. Promenades border the lawn, flanked by 52 Medjool date palms. The arbor features a water display designed to run off the roof in thin streams that flow into the fountain.

New Orleans City Park is a magnificent balance of art, nature and play, from its earliest designs intended to be "the happy medium betwixt the wildness of nature and the stiffness of art." But it is also an awesome juxtaposition of the ancient and the new, a dreamscape of 19th-, 20th-, and 21st-century innovation. It is an almost unbelievable triumph for those early advocates who envisioned a great park for a great city more than 150 years ago.

The Goldring-Woldenberg Great Lawn balances the old and new as a perfect metaphor for the park today. On one side a grand new fountain and arbor; on the other, the Peristyle, built in 1907.

People gather on the lawn with picnics and wine today to enjoy a concert and fireworks, almost exactly as New Orleanians did a hundred years ago. Beyond the symphony stage and the Peristyle, the dense, green canopy of the 800-year old oaks adds an echo of centuries long past.

The Goldring-Woldenberg Great Lawn is a beautiful place to play catch or bring a picnic for a symphony concert.

NOLA City Bark opened in 2010. City Park's doggie playground is an award-winning 4.6-acre off-leash dog park with an event lawn, quarter-mile walking trail, and separate play areas for small and big dogs.

This Page, Bottom: The Bead Dog in City Bark (photo courtesy of City Park)

City Park's Festival Grounds opened in 2012. The 50-acre green space has 5 sports fields, acres of wetlands, an exercise area with hydraulic fitness equipment, and a one-mile, 18-foot-wide path for walking, biking and jogging. The Reunion Shelter, a covered, open-air structure, is powered by 65 solar panels.

The Festival Grounds hosts large events like Hogs for the Cause and the Voodoo Music Experience.

Photo on this page by Brett Bazan

Another of the new/old attractions in City Park is miniature golf. The first mini golf course in the park opened in the 1920s. Today's City Putt is dotted with fanciful creations from Blaine Kern Artists, Inc., and landscaped with wonderful hills and water features. The 36-hole City Putt has two courses: the Louisiana Course highlights cultural themes and cities from around the state while the New Orleans Course showcases streets and iconic themes from around the city.

The park has emerged from its beginnings as a back-of-town escape to a front-and-center, major urban park. And it's not done. Looking to 2018, three hundred years after Bienville tromped through to start a unique town, the park has a master plan to expand and improve itself.

A new entrance to the Botanical Garden, a splash park to be known as City Splash, a skate park, a championship-level golf course and an environmental education center are all in the works.

In addition to the new Festival Grounds, the area north of Big Lake will have a children's museum. Miles of new hiking and bike paths will open up unseen vistas.

The plan also calls for an aggressive push not only to be a model of tree stewardship but to create a diverse and robust forest on the grounds, while providing an increased level of protection for the true natural treasure of the park—the stand of mature trees that symbolize New Orleans itself. Those live oaks, cypresses and magnolias are actual eyewitnesses to three centuries of her growth—from wild colonial outpost to vibrant world supercity.

Facing Page: A water feature in the miniature golf course, bronze cranes

Photo above by John Hopper

In 1995, City Park acquired Couba Island, roughly 4,000 acres of marsh and swamp with Lake Cataouatche to the north and Lake Salvador to the south. The island is about 19 miles southeast of City Park, outside New Orleans in St. Charles Parish. It is completely undeveloped, unoccupied and accessible only by boat. While City Park has no plans for development of the island for recreation, Couba is not much different from the City Park of the early 1800s or Couturie Forest today. Who knows what it might be in centuries to come.

Index

Facing Page, Bottom: *Windows* (1989) by John Scott, welded steel, on Golf Drive near the Christian Brothers School

This Page, Top: Voodoo concert photo by Brett Bazan
Bottom: photo by John Hopper

Facing Page: *Wave* (1988) kinetic sculpture by Lin Emery, polished aluminum, in the fountain at the entrance of the New Orleans Museum of Art

This Page, Top: Dog Day Afternoon Walk-a-thon and Festival benefiting the Louisiana SPCA happens on the lawn by Big Lake. Bottom: One of the Louisiana-themed creatures at City Putt, bronze gator.